Ouch! It Bit Me!

A Book about Interjections

by Cari Meister
illustrated by Holli Conger

Say Hello to Amicus Readers.

You'll find our helpful dog, Amicus, chasing a ball—to let you know the reading level of a book.

1

Learn to Read

High frequency words and close photo-text matches introduce familiar topics and provide support for brand new readers.

2

Read Independently

Some repetition is mixed with varied sentence structures and a select amount of new vocabulary words are introduced with text and photo support.

3

Read to Know More

Interesting facts and engaging art and photos give fluent readers fun books both for reading practice and to learn about new topics.

Amicus Readers are published by Amicus
P.O. Box 1329, Mankato, MN 56002
www.amicuspublishing.us

Illustrations by Holli Conger
Editor Wendy Dieker
Designer Heather Dreisbach

Printed in the United States of America.

10 9 8 7 6 5 4 3 2 1

Library of Congress Cataloging-in-Publication Data
Names: Meister, Cari, author. | Conger, Holli, illustrator.
Title: Ouch! it bit me! : a book about interjections / by Cari Meister ; illustrated by Holli Conger.
Description: Mankato, Minnesota : Amicus, [2017] | Say what? Parts of Speech. | Audience: K to Grade 3_
Identifiers: LCCN 2015041478 (print) | LCCN 2015046775 (ebook) | ISBN 9781607539322 (library binding) | ISBN 9781681510569 (eBook)
Subjects: LCSH: English language--Interjections--Juvenile literature. | English language--Parts of speech--Juvenile literature.
Classification: LCC PE1355 .M45 2017 (print) | LCC PE1355 (ebook) | DDC 428.2/4--dc23
LC record available at http://lccn.loc.gov/2015041478

An interjection is a word that shows emotions. The **purple** words in the story are interjections.

Bernard, Scarlett, and Nora are in the treehouse. "**Yikes!**" says Scarlett. "There's a spider on the wall."

“Wow!” says Bernard. “It’s huge!”

“Cool!” says Nora. “Let me hold it!”

"Ouch! It bit me," says Nora.

"Oh no!" says Scarlett. "I hope it's not poisonous."

Bernard catches the spider.

"Aha," he says. "Here is my spider book. Let's see what kind it is."

"It looks like this spider," he says. "Phew! It's not poisonous."

"Hooray!" says Scarlett.

The three friends go inside. Nora washes the bite. She puts ice on it.

"Well," she says, "that feels a lot better. I probably shouldn't try to hold spiders."

Bernard says, "I have to
go get, er, something."

He runs to his room.
Soon he is back.

"Hey!" he says. "Catch! This is one spider you can hold!"

"Oh my!" says Nora. "That's one big spider!"

Jobs of an Interjection

An interjection shows strong feelings or emotions.

Yikes! There's a spider on the wall.

Oh no! I hope it's not poisonous!

Interjections can show a pause.

I have to go get, er, something.